www.providencebooks.net

Publisher Contact

Email:contact@providencebooks.net

Social media: facebook.com/providencebooks

Acknowledgements

The team at Providence Books would like to thank our friends, family, suppliers and customers for making our vision of creating the highest-quality books a reality. Thanks for purchasing and enjoy the quotes!

This page is intentionally left blank

This page is intentionally left blank

'SNL' is really hard to do when you're single and living alone. And then it's pretty tough when you're married, because you don't see your spouse.

Bill Hader

'The State' was a huge thing for me. I watched that and 'SNL' together when I was 15, 16.

Bill Hader

'Vanity Fair' did this grid thing a couple years ago, connecting people who've worked together, and I had the most branches on it or whatever, because I'd worked with so-and-so and so-and-so worked with so-and-so, and I was kind of in the middle.

Bill Hader

A lot of times I think people, when they're doing a movie that's a family movie, they're worried about this being too esoteric or too dark or too weird.

Bill Hader

A person being patient with an insane person is my favorite thing in the world.

Bill Hader

As far as post-'SNL' career, whatever kind of comes my way that looks interesting, I'll do it, you know?

Bill Hader

At the beginning of each week at 'Saturday Night Live,' we have a full cast meeting where Lorne Michaels introduces the upcoming host.

Bill Hader

Before you get to 'SNL,' you have your own sensibility. And when you get to 'SNL,' it's the show's sensibility.

Bill Hader

Comedy is incredibly hard. You have to be loose. You have to be not afraid to fail.

Bill Hader

David Sedaris is so good that it makes me mad.

Bill Hader

Even though it doesn't look like it, I run. On a treadmill. And I bounce around to all the songs on my iPod - the Pixies, Wagner, Richard and Linda Thompson, even books on tape. Just not self-help ones.

Bill Hader

Every two months, I would get an email, 'Skeleton Twins update: still don't have the money!'

Bill Hader

Everything is so tech now; everyone is so connected that way.

Bill Hader

For our anniversary, my wife and I went to see Godzilla, and then we ate at Barnyard Venice, and it was like, 'We are crazy! The Kardashians have to keep up with us!'

Bill Hader

Fred Armisen does a pretty good me.

Bill Hader

Fred Willard still makes me laugh.

Bill Hader

George Saunders is a complete genius.

Bill Hader

Getting 'SNL' was pretty amazing, so just to be able to have an eight-year career there and be really happy with everything I did, it was pretty big.

Bill Hader

Going to any loud place is terrible for me. I'm bad at loud restaurants.

Bill Hader

Good directors give short and specific instructions to their actors.

Bill Hader

I - at the table reads, I break constantly. If something is up there that I'm not expecting, I tend to - I can't help myself; I'll start laughing.

Bill Hader

I can't do Twitter or Facebook, mostly because I feel like I'm the type of person who has to regiment the amount of time I spend doing certain things or I'll just wade in it, and then I'll never come out.

Bill Hader

I collect movies. So I have all those in binders. I don't have the DVDs out. I put them in binders.

Bill Hader

I don't believe in the term 'guilty pleasure,' because it implies I should feel ashamed for liking something. A real guilty pleasure would be, I don't know, taking gratification in some stranger's ghastly death or something - which I guess I do enjoy, because I read a ton of true crime.

Bill Hader

I don't think I could do what Woody Allen or Clint Eastwood or Ben Stiller do, where they direct a movie and they star in it. I would just be like, 'Oh, I don't even want to look at my face.'

Bill Hader

I get migraines a lot. I get them when I'm stressed out. My brain freezes, and I just try to get through that.

Bill Hader

I got invited to the Playboy Mansion with the Lonely Island guys after their first season on 'SNL,' and I sat in the corner drinking coffee and talking to Akiva Schaffer about what aspect ratio he was going to shoot 'Hot Rod' in. Like, that's what we talk about.

Bill Hader

I grew up in a total Pink Floyd house.

Bill Hader

I grew up with my two sisters and my mom, so it's my lot in life to be surrounded by women.

Bill Hader

I had a small part in 'Pineapple Express.'

Bill Hader

I hated pitch meetings. Pitch meetings were my least favorite part of the week. I just gave up. I was so terrible at them.

Bill Hader

I have a lot of incomplete short films and incomplete scripts out there.

Bill Hader

I just did this movie with Kristin Wiig called 'The Skeleton Twins.' That's a straight drama. We play estranged twins, and I end up moving in with her and her husband, played by Luke Wilson. But it's a drama, and the Duplass Brothers produced it and this great guy, Craig Johnson, directed it. And that was great, you know?

Bill Hader

I kind of romanticized what it was like to be a writer and director when I was in my early twenties. Working as a production assistant knocked that right out of me.

Bill Hader

I learned a lot just watching people perform.

Bill Hader

I like doing a lot of research, and then you get there, you're in wardrobe, and then you're just reacting to what the other person is doing. The other actor is reacting to what you're doing, and it's this great back and forth. Because you've done all this research, you can use some of it or throw a lot of it out. You can get lost in it.

Bill Hader

I like watching Kate McKinnon do something - there's a joy in seeing a new move from somebody and going, 'Oh, she can do that.'

Bill Hader

I like when you are telling a story and fall into an impression.

Bill Hader

I love comedy, but it's dramas that stick with me.

Bill Hader

I met Robin Williams a few times, and he was a beautiful guy.

Bill Hader

I moved out to L.A. to be a filmmaker or director. I didn't even think about doing comedy or even acting. I wanted to be like Paul Thomas Anderson or Wes Anderson, but I wasn't going to a lot of comedy.

Bill Hader

I really enjoyed playing Vinny Vedecci, the Italian talk show host. He was the first character I ever came up with where I gave him a name and a way of dressing.

Bill Hader

I really liked John Candy in 'Planes, Trains & Automobiles.' He was so good in that movie.

Bill Hader

I remember I could do - I did Bart Simpson once on the bus. I did, like, a really good Bart Simpson voice on the bus, obviously before I hit puberty. And everybody went, 'Whoa, that sounds just like Bart Simpson.'

Bill Hader

I remember being unbelievable bummed when 'Freaks and Geeks' was canceled.

Bill Hader

I remember seeing 'Spinal Tap' at a young age and being like, 'That's how you perform comedy.'

Bill Hader

I saw 'A Clockwork Orange' when I was 11. When you watch 'Clockwork Orange' at 11, it either totally scares you from watching movies, or you want to become a filmmaker. I was the latter.

Bill Hader

I set the time on my iPhone to be 30 minutes late, so I'm only an hour and a half late to appointments now.

Bill Hader

I started 'SNL,' and I became the one who did impressions. I did that, but then I wanted to get an original character on, and that took a long time to get one on that stuck. And then I got Vinny Vedecci on - 'Oh great' - and then it took a couple more seasons to get Greg the Alien on. You have to have some patience.

Bill Hader

I started making little short films with friends, and then I decided I wanted to get into the school play in high school.

Bill Hader

I think that's the thing I learned at 'Saturday Night Live' - any time I would try and strategize, I would always, always fall on my face. Things worked out when I tried to make it about what I was feeling at that moment and what I was into in that moment of my life.

Bill Hader

I took Second City out of desperation, and that's what ended up working out. It shows that you should be doing a lot of different stuff, taking whatever opportunities are there, to see what works.

Bill Hader

I tried to get people at 'South Park' into 'Downton Abbey,' and it didn't work. I think they were like, "Downton Abbey?' What?' And I kinda made a big plea in the writer's room, like, 'Guys, you should really watch it. It's good. It's addicting. My wife and I are obsessed with it.'

Bill Hader

I was a production assistant in the post department on 'The Surreal Life.' And it's been reported before that I was an assistant editor on 'The Surreal Life.' That is not true.

Bill Hader

I was always self-conscious about the fact that I didn't have as much comedy experience as other people at 'SNL,' and I kept thinking they were going to realize they'd made a mistake by hiring me.

Bill Hader

I was at Second City L.A., going through the conservatory, and I graduated in 2004 and I got 'SNL' in 2005.

Bill Hader

I was in a sketch group in L.A., and we were playing, like, backyards in Glendale and stuff. It was pretty ugly because we didn't have any money.

Bill Hader

I was never that good on stage with live improv. I was much better on film or writing something and then thinking about it. I was too in my head when I was on stage.

Bill Hader

I was offered a lot of supporting crazy parts in comedies because that's all I had done.

Bill Hader

I work a lot, and it's kind of like, you meet people, and you just click. It's not like I'm looking at something and thinking: "South Park' - how do I get on that?' I just became friends with those guys first. They're nice guys.

Bill Hader

I worked at a movie theater in Tempe, Arizona, when I went to community college there. And I got fired because a sorority had rented out a theater to watch 'Titanic,' and they were being really rude to me while they were waiting for the movie. So as I tore their tickets, I told them the end of the movie.

Bill Hader

I would do 'Superbad,' and the next offers you would get would all be crazy cop characters or crazy security guards or something.

Bill Hader

I would say it wasn't until my fourth season on 'SNL' where people or my agent was saying, 'You're an actor.' I never thought of it that way.

Bill Hader

I wrote a fan e-mail to Michael Chabon.

Bill Hader

I'm a huge fan of Simon Pegg and Nick Frost.

Bill Hader

I'm always up before everybody else. I also crash at 3 o'clock when everybody's at their prime.

Bill Hader

I'm crazy lucky. I was trying to be a filmmaker. I was doing Second City classes as a way to be creative. I was a PA for a long time. I was working as an assistant editor on 'Iron Chef America' when I got 'SNL.' It was one of those situations where you're concentrating in one thing and the peripheral thing popped.

Bill Hader

I'm never going to say, 'Well, I'm never going to do comedy again.' I love comedies, and it's what people know me for, so I love doing it... I don't really think about it in terms of 'Well, I should do this because it's comedy or drama.'

Bill Hader

I'm the only one in Tulsa, Oklahoma, that has Final Draft on my computer. Then you show up and go to any coffee shop in L.A., and there are a hundred people your age with Final Draft.

Bill Hader

I'm very close to my sisters.

Bill Hader

I've always admired Jeff Bridges. I really like how one can never get a handle on what he's doing.

Bill Hader

I've been a big fan of David Wain's and was honored to get to be in one of his projects.

Bill Hader

I've never met Charlie Sheen.

Bill Hader

I've seen people who come to work say, 'No, I'm doing it this way, and that's that.' I'm the opposite - I like being out of my element; it's where I like to live.

Bill Hader

If I get a chance to write a comic book or do a voice in an Adult Swim show, I do it. It's much more fulfilling to me and I get to work with people who I'm a fan of.

Bill Hader

If a movie doesn't even have financing yet, they'll do a table read for it at a casting director's office with actors, for the producer and the writer, just to hear if the movie is working.

Bill Hader

If you can't forgive yourself, you think you're never going to be able to forgive yourself, and you repeat the same behavior.

Bill Hader

If you watch 'SNL,' any time there's this thing with everyone singing, I'm, like, the one person who just has a straight line of dialogue because I can't sing to save my life.

Bill Hader

In 'Winter's Bone,' it's literally the director and the camera operator. That's it. Just a super-small Kubrick crew. You know what I mean? Like, 8 people.

Bill Hader

In the U.S., it's like, you start with a great script, and then on set - not everybody, but definitely in the Apatow group - you go off, and you're improvising on camera. So while you're on camera, you're saying things that no one else has ever heard before during the actual take.

Bill Hader

It doesn't occur to me that I don't drive a cool car until I hang out with Jon Hamm, who picks me up in what looks like a Transformer, and I think, 'Oh, that's what movie stars are driving. I guess I'm not a movie star.'

Bill Hader

It is funny that people always assume you have a bigger part in a movie than you actually do. I remember a lot of people thought 'Adventureland' starred me and Kristen Wiig. But we were like, 'No, we're only in the movie for like ten minutes!'

Bill Hader

Jason Sudeikis is always chewing gum.

Bill Hader

Jon Ronson makes me laugh. I've read all of his books.

Bill Hader

Las Vegas, New Mexico has had a lot of great movies shot there.

Bill Hader

Let's face it: I look pretty out of shape.

Bill Hader

My dad was a big Frank Zappa fan, so I remember listening to a lot of Frank Zappa. Girls do not like Frank Zappa.

Bill Hader

My first real job, I sold Christmas trees when I was twelve for extra money. I did that until I was fifteen. Then I bagged groceries, and I worked at the first Borders ever in Tulsa, Oklahoma.

Bill Hader

My life is different since I moved back to L.A. from New York, mostly because I have a family and I don't go out.

Bill Hader

My mom, dad, grandparents, we all do voices.

Bill Hader

My parents were supportive. I didn't have good grades, but they could tell I wasn't lazy.

Bill Hader

My wife and I got to go onstage at a Flaming Lips concert at Webster Hall once. We dressed up like Scientology aliens and danced around. We had a shootout onstage with Santa Claus.

Bill Hader

My wife and I were on our honeymoon in Turks and Caicos, in the middle of nowhere, and I'm sitting on this deserted beach, and I see one lone person walking along the shore. He walks right up to me and says, 'I love 'Laser Cats,'' and then just walks away.

Bill Hader

My wife is the sweetest, most even-keeled person ever. A mood swing to her is like, 'Oh, I'm uncomfortable.'

Bill Hader

Oddly enough, I have really bad stage fright - getting up in front of people. And I made a living going on live television.

Bill Hader

One of the reasons I started working at 'South Park,' actually, was that I wanted to learn how to structure things and how to tell a story.

Bill Hader

Paul Rudd is a huge 'Hot Rod' fan.

Bill Hader

People ask me, 'Did you always want to be on SNL?' No, actually, it never crossed my mind. It didn't even seem possible. It would've been like saying, 'Hey, do you wanna go to the moon?'

Bill Hader

Pete Davidson - he's in the movie 'Trainwreck.' He has a small part in it. I told Lorne Michaels about him, said he was really funny.

Bill Hader

Seth Meyers and I wrote a 'Spider-Man' comic.

Bill Hader

Sometimes you're working with somebody, and you can tell they're just waiting to say their line.

Bill Hader

The first time I ever acted was in 'The Glass Menagerie' in high school, and my first line was, 'I didn't know Shakespeare had a sister.'

Bill Hader

The first time I met James Franco, he was dressed like James Dean. He was James Dean, literally, filming a biopic.

Bill Hader

The nature of 'SNL' is that it's so in-the-moment.

Bill Hader

The whole thing with animated movies is that it's very hard to get out of your head because it's very moving through each line systematically.

Bill Hader

There are some really funny women at 'SNL,' man.

Bill Hader

There's a movie called 'Pod People' that has a weird little anteater alien. That was a good alien.

Bill Hader

To be honest, I don't know how comedy works.

Bill Hader

To be honest, I watch way more dramatic films when I'm chilling at home. I think when you work in comedy, you just want something different in your private life. Makes you feel balanced, I guess.

Bill Hader

To be totally honest? I don't know if I'll keep doing more impressions. People told me I had a facility for it, and I was like, 'Okay, I'm the impression guy.' So you imagine the cast at 'SNL' is an A-Team, and you've got the explosives guy, and I'm the impression guy.

Bill Hader

Top Ten lists make me insane. I just know they're going to change daily.

Bill Hader

Turns out typecasting is a real thing.

Bill Hader

Voices are a good way to get in and out of things. James Carville constantly calls my wife to say I'll be home late. Mandy Patinkin and Al Pacino call to get me restaurant reservations.

Bill Hader

When 'MacGruber' came out, David Wain was one of the first people who publicly championed it.

Bill Hader

When I got to 'Saturday Night Live,' it was a lot like going from pre-school to Harvard, and it took a long time to figure stuff out.

Bill Hader

When I met Judd Apatow, he told me I should start writing screenplays. They'd be really bad at first, but the more I did it, the better I'd get.

Bill Hader

When I was on 'SNL,' I was getting weirdly anxious about being on camera, which I had never really done before. And so my solution was just to not watch my stuff. And then I found out that other actors do it, too, and I felt less weird about it.

Bill Hader

When it comes to comedy, it might be interesting to know why an airplane works, but really? Maybe it's better not to know why certain things work. Just fly the thing, and if nothing falls apart, you'll be fine.

Bill Hader

When people tell you what doesn't work, they're usually right. When they tell you how to fix it, they're usually wrong.

Bill Hader

When you move to L.A. or New York, it's easy to get a little lost and forget your original goal.

Bill Hader

When you saw Jon Lovitz or Dana Carvey or Phil Hartman doing something, they were acting. It was real acting. Like, they were acting like that person. They weren't like - it wasn't even like they were really trying to go for a laugh, especially in Phil Hartman's case.

Bill Hader

When you're at your absolute, most exhausted... That's when you have to be at the top of your game.

Bill Hader

When you're performing, you're playing to the back row. With acting, you have to be more nuanced.

Bill Hader

Yeah, improvising only really works 100% when you're with somebody.

Bill Hader

You can be the lead in a movie just for the sake of being a lead in a movie, or you can just be in a good movie.

Bill Hader

You know what, I remember being on my T-ball team and telling people about 'Platoon.'

Bill Hader

You learn quickly at 'SNL' you get in trouble if you compare yourself to other people, where they're at, or what other people had done before you.

Bill Hader

This page is intentionally left blank

This page is intentionally left blank

This page is intentionally left blank

This page is intentionally left blank

This page is intentionally left blank

www.ingramcontent.com/pod-product-compliance
Lightning Source LLC
Chambersburg PA
CBHW061933280526
45787CB00004B/1593